BEAUTIFUL ME

WRITTEN BY
CHIOMA LINDO

ILLUSTRATED BY
SHELLENE RODNEY

Illustrated by Shellene Rodney

Chioma Lindo, the author of Beautiful Me, is the owner of Jones & Zuri LLC. Visit jonesandzuri.com for information on the company, workshops, products, and more.

Printed in the United States of America

First printing, 2017

Library of Congress Control Number: 2017958891

Soft cover: ISBN 978-1-945091-60-5
Hard cover: ISBN 978-1-945091-61-2

Ordering information: Special discounts are available on quantity purchases by bookstores, corporations, associations, and others. For details, contact the publisher at:

sales@braughlerbooks.com
or at 937-58-BOOKS

For questions or comments about this book, please write to:

info@braughlerbooks.com

Braughler™
Books
braughlerbooks.com

My inspiration for this book

Zuri Isabel ❤ Dr. M. Lindo ❤ Shannon Hoefler

Dear parents, guardians, and caretakers;

The definition of beauty: a. the quality of being physically attractive b. the qualities in a person or a thing that give pleasure to the senses or the mind.

Beautiful Me was created to help little girls identify and embrace the positive attributes, inside and out, that shape them and that the unique combination is a part of their beauty.

It is our goal to celebrate a broader concept of beauty and we want your little one, from the earliest time in her life, to know that she is beautiful!

Join this gang (McKenzie, Vivian, Ella, Haley, Ava, Zuri)
as they explore all the great things
that make us different yet beautiful.

I am beautiful...   and I am beautiful...

...because we are not you.

But wait, you are beautiful too!

We are beautiful with our different shapes, sizes...

...and colors.

or something else all together.

And what about those eyes?
Can't imagine them any other color.

That's not it. That's not all my friend.

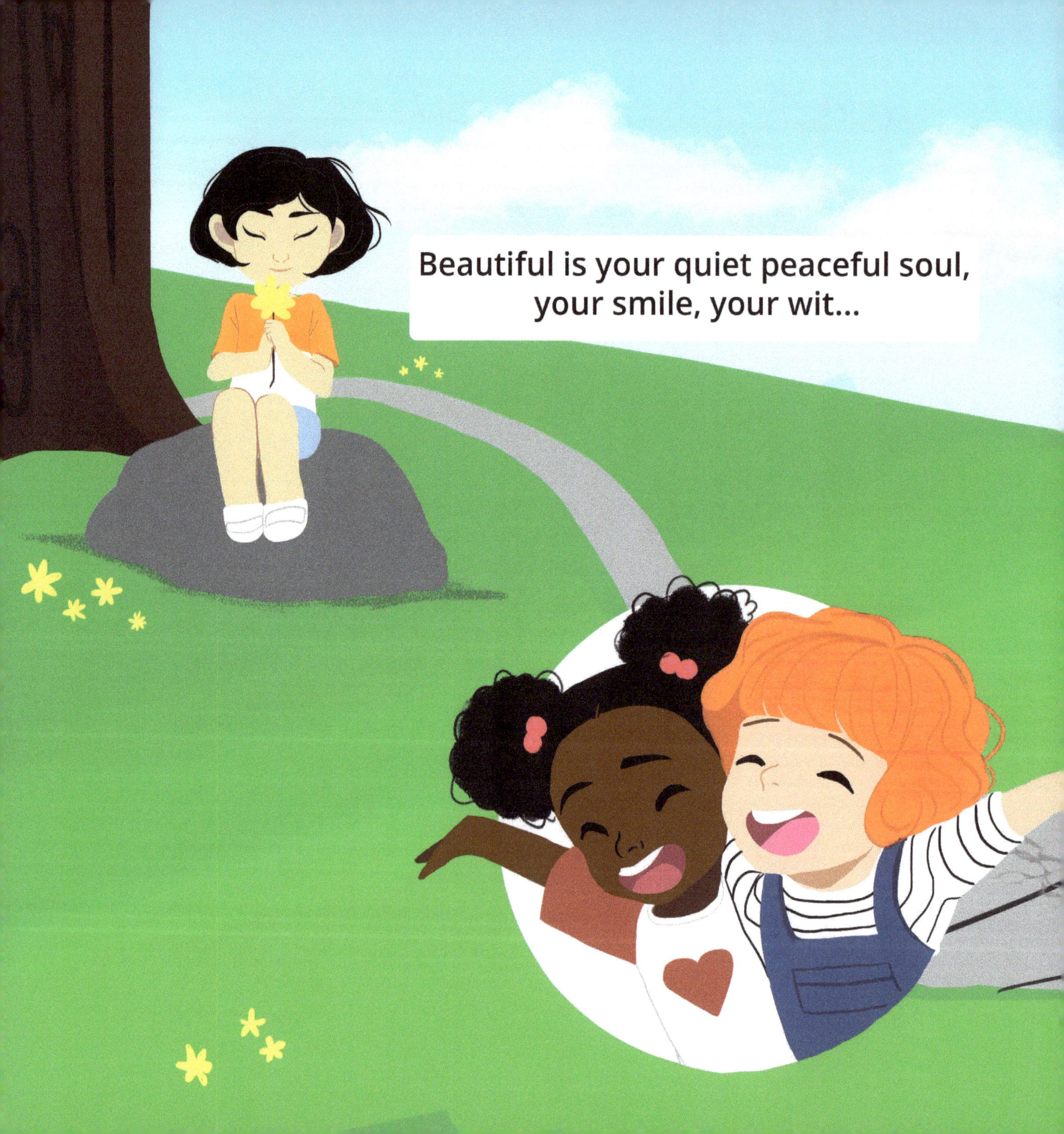
Beautiful is your quiet peaceful soul,
your smile, your wit...

...or your **BOLD** and carefree spirit.

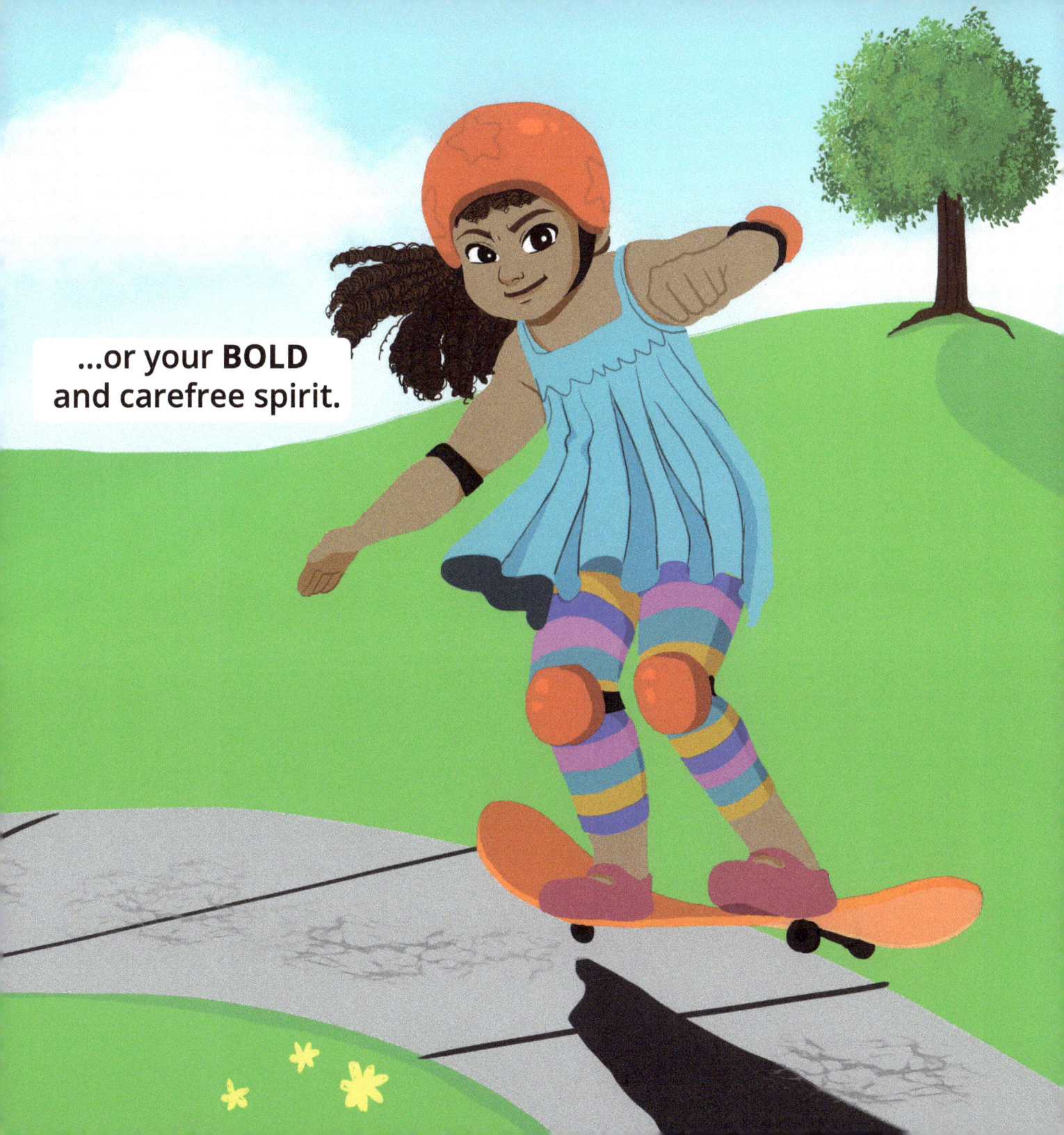

Beautiful is
your helping hands,

your praying knees...

and the way you help those in need.

Beautiful is
the hugs you give,
the dance moves you create,
and the songs you sing
that make this world a happier place.

There is more! Beautiful is...

The shoulder you give to cry on, that kindness in your heart...

Bonjour

Здравствуйте

你好

and all the ways you can greet those around you.

こんにちは

Olá

Hola

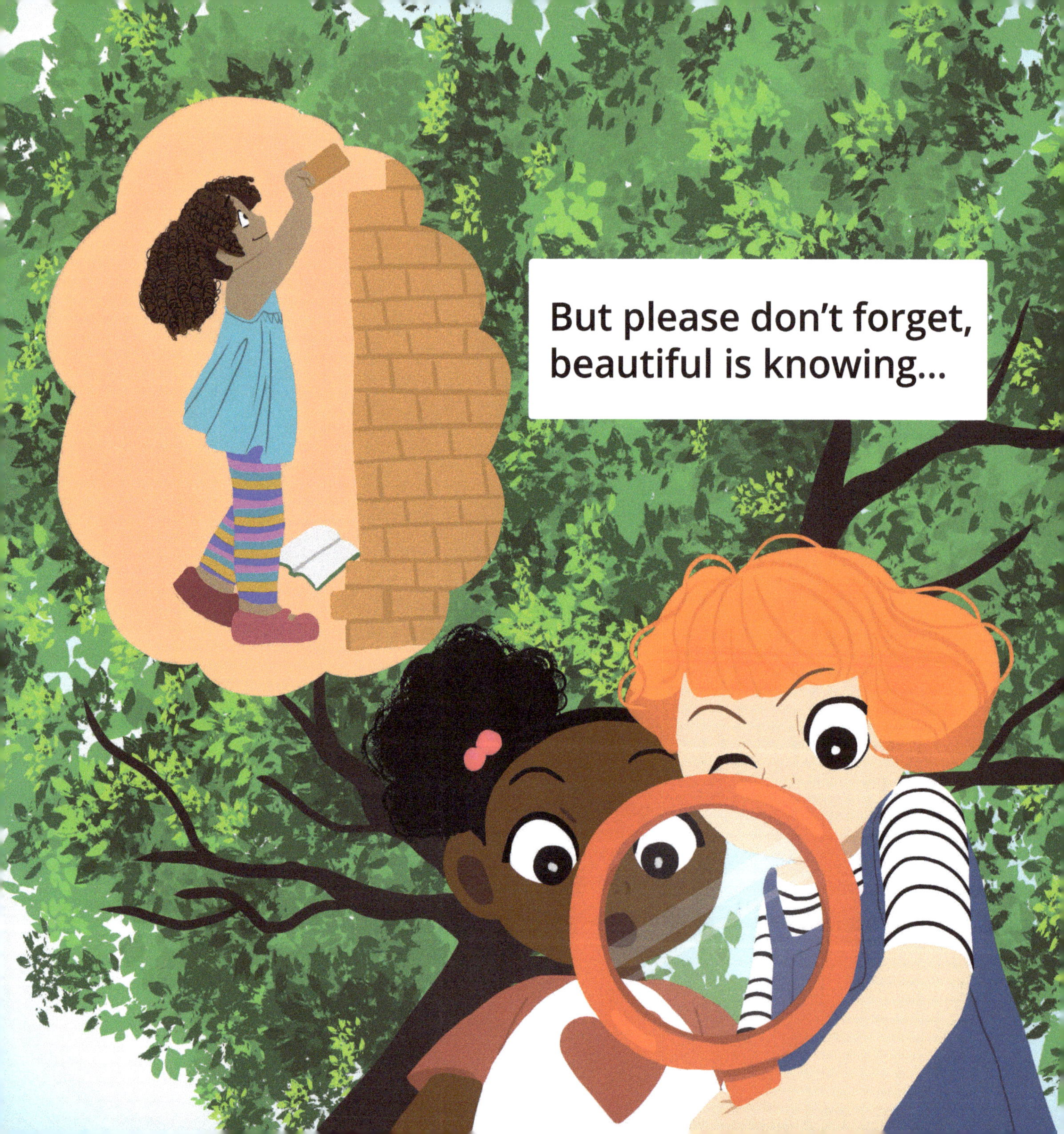
But please don't forget,
beautiful is knowing...

YOU ARE SMART!

Hmmm, what else did we forget?

Oh yes!
Be glad that I look different from you
and you look different from me.

If we all looked and acted the same
how boring that would be.

I am beautiful.   And I am beautiful...

because we are not you.
But always remember this, you are beautiful too.

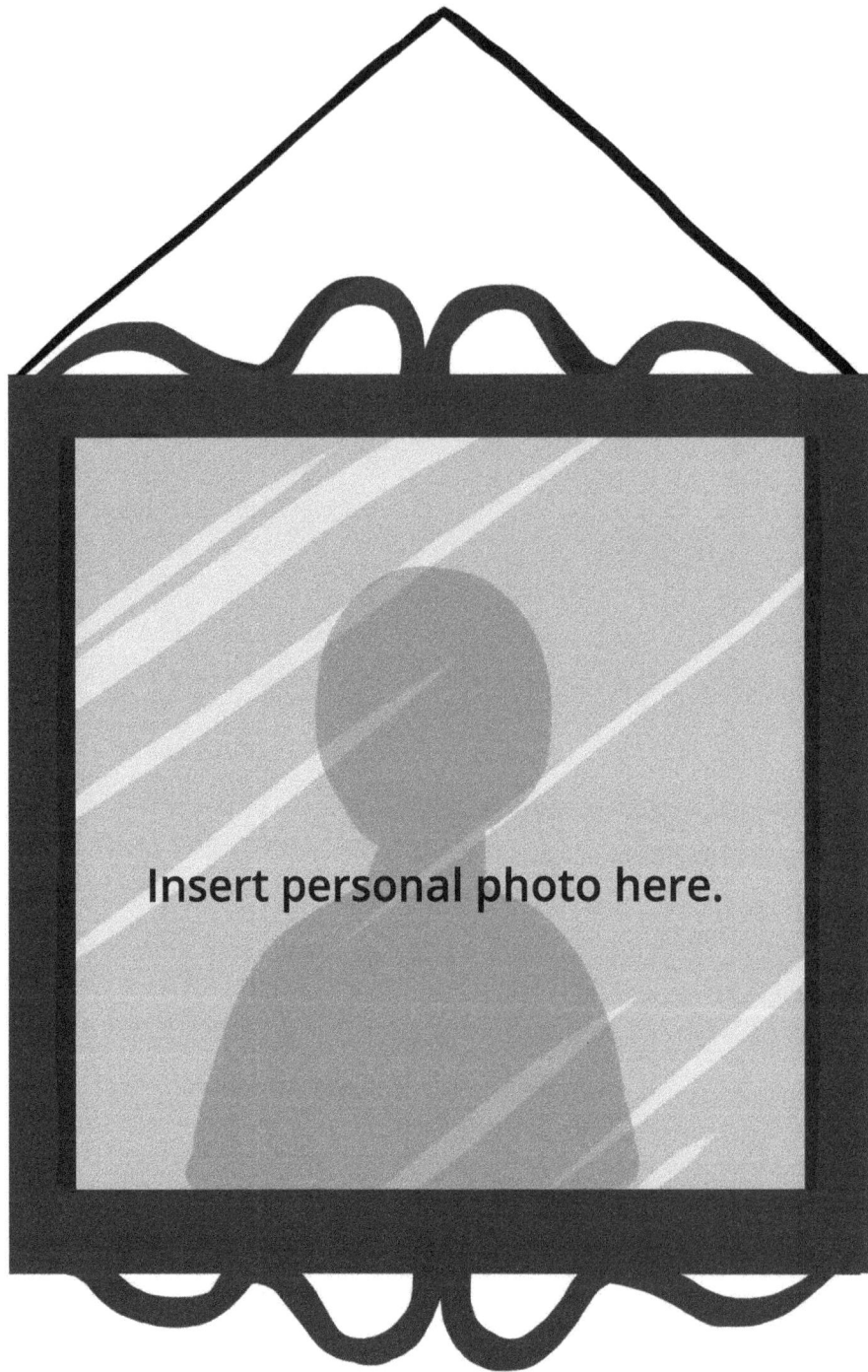

Insert personal photo here.

What makes you beautiful?

_____

_____

_____

_____

_____

_____

_____

_____

_____

_____

_____

_____

_____

_____

_____

_____

_____

_____

_____

_____

Were you able to identify all the ways to say hello?

Bonjour - French

Здравствуйте - Russian

你好 - Mandarin

こんにちは - Punjabi

Olá - Portuguese

Hola - Spanish

www.ingramcontent.com/pod-product-compliance
Lightning Source LLC
LaVergne TN
LVHW070835080426

835508LV00031B/3468